Down Syndrome, Blessed with *ThisAbility*

NOW IMAGINE LIFE WITHOUT ME

D1196953

Craig Woodard Sr.

Lisa Mezzei

Jennifer Quinn

Tahira Myers

Megan McGee

Lawrence Bach

Melissa Miner

ISBN 978-1-64559-832-9 (Paperback)
ISBN 978-1-64559-833-6 (Digital)

Covenant Books, Inc.
11661 Hwy 707
Murrells Inlet, SC 29576
www.covenantbooks.com

My name is Craig Woodard Sr., and a couple of years ago, I had this idea of getting together with other families who have children blessed with Down syndrome and write a book about our journey. I asked each willing parent to write a chapter about their unique experiences so that we had a wide variety of real life examples to share with other parents who are expecting or have had a child blessed with Down syndrome.

I shared my story of our experience with Craig Junior. The other writers who shared my vision are Lisa Mezzei, Jennifer Quinn, Tahira Myers, Megan McGee, Lawrence Bach, and Melissa Miner. These parents are all exceptional parents with different stories that are beautiful and special in their own right. I want to thank all six of these individuals for taking the time to allow everyone into your world for just a moment. Your generosity and unselfishness will assist many other families along the way in one of the most important decisions in their lives.

The point of this book is to give parents who are pregnant with or have had a child blessed with Down syndrome an inside look at the good times and the tough times. It's challenging raising kids, period, but we all want you to know that everything will be all right. These individuals born with Down syndrome are so special in our eyes. So special that the Quinn family adopted four angels blessed with Trisomy 21.

Termination rates are still extremely high, and this book will help shed some light on how life is with a child born with Down syndrome. Enter into our lives, and share in our journey. When you meet our angels, you will see how special these individuals are. You will notice that these children don't have a "disability," they were born with "ThisAbility."

What is "ThisAbility?"

ThisAbility is the term that I replaced disability with. Disability, in my opinion, sounds like something negative. People view it as negative, different or not fully capable. I don't view it in that fashion. Each and every individual that was born with a special need or who became disabled after birth was given the gift of being blessed with ThisAbility. These individuals have ThisAbility to bring people of different races, backgrounds and way of life together. They have ThisAbility to put a smile on people's faces. They have ThisAbility to love those that often are discriminating against them. These special angels have ThisAbility to make this a kinder, gentler world.

Each individual was blessed with a unique way they can touch the people in the world around them. That's an extremely positive thing. I see nothing negative about it. I challenge you to look at someone with special needs as your equal. Treat everyone the same. Make sure you give yourself the opportunity to see the greatness that they bestow. If you do this and you stay true to this process, you will be blessed. You will see ThisAbility and you will marvel at how individuals faced with life's challenges go about life everyday with their heads held high and a smile on their faces. They have ThisAbility and will change the world one conversation at a time. All of the kiddos mentioned in this book have ThisAbility and if your child is blessed with Down syndrome, they will have ThisAbility as well.

Contents

Introduction

"There's a strong possibility that your child will be born with Down syndrome!"—these are the words that many of us have heard at some point during our pregnancies. Some of us did not hear these words and had no warning. How are you supposed to feel? How are you supposed to react? It's a wide range of emotions that most parents go through. We, at Down Syndrome Association of Tampa Bay (DSATB), can relate to what you are going through and what you are about to go through. We are a Down syndrome organization in the Tampa Bay area that reaches out to families across the bay in order to educate and support those who are getting ready to have a child with Down syndrome or who have already given birth to that special angel.

My name is Craig Woodard Sr., and I'm one of the founders of DSATB. My team and I started DSATB on February 23, 2018, and I was named the executive director and president. I wanted to get involved because my son was born with Down syndrome in April 2014. According to the Centers for Disease Control and Prevention, approximately one in every seven hundred babies in the United States is born with Down syndrome. About six thousand babies are born with Down syndrome each year in the United States. There's roughly a 90 percent abortion rate after parents find out from prenatal screenings that they may have a child with Down syndrome. 90 percent—this number is incredibly high! *This has to change.*

Down syndrome is a chromosomal disorder also known as Trisomy 21. Each child gets twenty-three chromosomes from both parents. Children with Down syndrome have an extra twenty-first chromosome, giving them a total of forty-seven chromosomes instead of forty-six. The disorder can cause mental and physical delays, possible heart defects, and a weaker muscular structure.

In this book, you are going to hear from many of the families in the Tampa Bay area who are a part of the DSATB organization. We will share our very own personal experiences with you and show you how blessed we are to have our child, who was born with Down syndrome, in our lives. Our goal is to reduce the staggering 90 percent abortion rate through education and real-life stories!

The Woodard Family

Let me start off our journey with my very own family. My name is Craig Woodard Sr. and my lovely wife is Christine Woodard. I have two older sons from a prior marriage named Dante' and Jordan Woodard. Christine and I were blessed to give birth to our son, Craig Woodard Jr., on April 13, 2014. Junior was born with Down syndrome. Here is how it all began. Christine and I were college sweethearts, but we went to different schools. We met back in 1994 in Indiana, Pennsylvania, the day after my cousin got married. We exchanged phone numbers and I told her that I would call her. She went to school at Indiana University of Pennsylvania while I attended Mercyhurst University in Erie, Pennsylvania. We dated for just under a year, but the distance ended up playing a factor in our relationship, so we ended up going our separate ways. We both moved on, I got married and had Dante' and Jordan, and some years later, I got divorced. Back in 2008, Christine sent me a friend request on Facebook. It was good to hear from her, so I accepted. We never really said anything to one another on Facebook until she saw that I was going through a divorce. We ended up reconnecting, and I told her that I would never let her get away again. The good Lord has given us a second chance.

I proposed to her on September 10, 2010, and exactly one year to the day later on September 10, 2011, we got married. This was Christine's first marriage, and she had no children, so we started our lives together at a later age. I was thirty-six years old, and she was thirty-seven at the time. Both Christine and I talked about having a child. I had two kids already, and I loved the fact that she wanted to have a child with me. We began family planning, and shortly after we got married, we found out that we were pregnant. We both were so excited.

We went through some ups and downs early in the pregnancy. Chrissy went to the doctor for the first time and received shocking news. The doctor told her that there was no heartbeat. We were devastated. We set up another appointment, and when we went to the doctor, we found out that there was in fact a heartbeat and a fetal pole. The doctor then confirmed our pregnancy but told us not to get our hopes up. We had another appointment only a few days later, and when we attended that appointment, we found out that we did, in fact, lose the baby. The doctor gave us a private moment, and we just held each other and cried for what seemed like an eternity.

After we collected ourselves, I told Chrissy that we would keep trying to have a baby, and when the time is right, the Lord will bless us with a special angel. The emotional roller coaster wasn't over with just yet. Chrissy was twelve weeks into her pregnancy when she lost our first baby, so she had to schedule what's called a D&C, also known as a dilation and curettage. This procedure removes tissue and clears the uterine lining after a miscarriage. It was another setback for us emotionally, but we made it through the procedure. After a couple of months, it was safe for us to start family planning once again.

We took our time, tried to remain stress free, and just let things happen naturally. In August of 2013, Chrissy took a pregnancy test. It came out positive. We were thrilled, but cautious. We called the doctor and set up an appointment so that they could confirm whether Chrissy was pregnant or not. When we went to the doctor, we were able to see the fetal pole, and we heard a strong heartbeat as well. What a great feeling that was. We both were very emotional. We hugged and kissed each other as we cried tears of happiness. We also knew that we had a long road ahead of us. Since Chrissy turned forty years old and she would give birth at the age of forty-one, we knew she was considered high risk. We had to change doctors, and we were referred to Florida Perinatal Associates, and we saw Dr. Craig Kalter. They had all of the high tech equipment there, and we knew we would be in good hands.

At one of Chrissy's appointments, she had to do blood work. When the results came in, they told us that there is a strong possibility that we could have a child born with Down syndrome. This seemed like another setback for us. We had no idea what Down syndrome was, and the doctor's office told us all that *could* happen to our child. We were told that 90 percent of parents that find out they may have a child with Down syndrome decide to terminate the pregnancy. The reason why is because of the developmental and intellectual delays that the child may have.

We were also told that there is possibility that our child may be born with a hole in his/her heart and may need to have open heart surgery to repair it. We heard all of this information, and we only had a small window to make a decision as to whether we wanted to continue the pregnancy or terminate. Well, termination for us was out of the question. This was another emotional roller coaster for us. The doctor told us that they could do a procedure called an amniocentesis. This is where they take a needle, insert it into the amniotic sac, and draw out some of the amniotic fluid and test it. There is a .6 percent chance of miscarriage by having this procedure done, but experienced facilities that perform this procedure regularly have rates closer to one in four hundred where miscarriages can occur.

Dr. Kalter gave Chrissy and I time to speak privately about whether we wanted to go through with the amniocentesis. We talked about it, shed a few tears, and decided it was better for us to find out now then to wait until the day the baby is born. Doctor Kalter came back into the room, and we told him that we wanted to go ahead and do the procedure now. We were able to see everything on the 3D monitor. It was very scary and painful, but we knew this was our choice. We saw the needle enter the amniotic sac, and the baby was on the other side of the sac nowhere near the needle, so he was away from any harm. However, if he moved abruptly, he could have hit the needle and that could have cause major damage or even death. Dr. Kalter did a fantastic job, and he retrieved enough fluid to perform his test. When the results came in, Dr. Kalter told us that the amniocentesis is showing a high likelihood that we were going to have a child with Down syndrome. At this point, we put our child in God's hands as we went on throughout the pregnancy, knowing what to expect when our child is born.

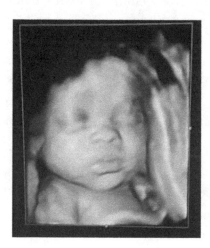

We had a four-dimension sonogram done and it was incredible. We could see his little face, his nose, his eyes, and his perfect little lips. From that point on, we fell in love with this little angel. When the baby started moving in Chrissy's belly, she would take my hand and put it on the area of her stomach where he was moving. It was the coolest thing ever. I used to sing to her belly every night, and the baby would move all around inside. He was a very active child inside of the womb. Chrissy went through a ton of morning sickness in her first and second trimesters. She was very miserable because of that, but she continued to work full-time up until the Friday before she gave birth. All her stress tests were good, and things progressed nicely as we got closer to her due date.

She was actually due on April 14, 2014. Since she was high risk, and because there was a strong possibility that the baby may have Down syndrome, the doctor scheduled a date where they would induce labor. It was the day before she went full term with the pregnancy, April 13, 2014. On Friday, April 11, Chrissy and I went to her regularly scheduled stress test in the afternoon. For the first time, the baby wasn't as active as he had been in past stress tests. The nurse sent a sound wave through the womb to wake the baby up, just in case he was sleeping or relaxing. This got his attention, and he started moving around a bit more, and we were able to increase our kick count. We were scheduled to come back to the hospital on Sunday, April 13, at 3:00 pm. We got there right at three o'clock, checked in and they took us back to our room. They began to do a stress test to make sure the baby was still very active.

They also let us hear the heartbeat. After about an hour and a half, the nurse went and got the doctor, and he came in to check the baby. We knew something was wrong because the nurses started to move faster, and the room got silent. The doctor was trying to find the heartbeat, and he was having problems finding it. He finally found it but said words that we weren't expecting to hear. He said, "Let's prepare to have an emergency C-section." *A cesarean section, but why?* I asked myself. This is a surgery where they cut through the wall of the mother's abdomen in order to remove the baby from the womb. The nurse came over to me and handed me a gown and a hair net to put on. They did this as they rushed my wife out of the room. She began to cry, and I just told her everything would be okay. I tried to text my mother and my mother-in-law in order to let them know that something was wrong, so we were having an emergency C-section.

I then had to leave my phone in the room while they took me to the operating room. They had given Chrissy an epidural and gave her pain medicine prior to the procedure. Chrissy gets sick every time she takes certain pain medications. When I came in the operating room, Chrissy was laying in the bed sick to her stomach. They began the C-section. It didn't take long for them to take the baby out. Dr. Foster held the baby and confirmed it was a boy. She stopped and allowed me to take his first picture after birth. He was crying, so we knew he was okay, or so we thought. After the picture, the doctor was clearing out his lungs and cleaning him off, and we heard her say he had a collapsed lung. They rushed him out of the operating room and took him to the neonatal intensive care unit.

This was such an uncomfortable position to be in. My wife was on the operating table, and they still had to close her back up. Our son had been rushed out of the room and taken to another part of the hospital, and then I was being told that I needed to go back to the room, get our things, and a nurse would come get me to take me to Chrissy in the recovery once her surgery was complete. I gathered our things, went to the cafeteria, and called my mom, my mother-in-law, and my dad to let them know what was going on. What a range of emotions! About thirty minutes later, a nurse came to get me, and she took me to see Chrissy in the recovery room.

She was still a bit sick to her stomach, and it took some time before she started getting movement back in her lower extremities. After a while, they took us up to the room that she would be in for the next few days. Chrissy's room was up on the fifth floor while the neonatal intensive care unit was on the second floor. Once I got in the room with Chrissy, I checked to see how she was doing. She was exhausted and sore, but doing okay. I told her that I was going to go down and check on the baby.

Prior to giving birth, we decided that we would name our son Craig Anthony Woodard, Jr. It was time that I went to pay Craig Junior. a visit, so off to the second floor I went. I was nervous, scared, excited, and protective all at the same time. As I got off the elevator and walked down the hallway, I had a sense of pride about myself. I couldn't wait to see my son. When I got to his room, the nurse was still in there, and my eyes went directly to him. She told me that his lung had already inflated on its own and that he was a bit jaundice, so to treat him, they had him under the bili lights (also known as phototherapy), and he had a hard plastic cover over his bed. He had a mask on that covered his eyes and all of these wires on his chest. It was extremely emotional for me to see my son like this. They assured me that he was fine.

I washed my hands thoroughly then dried them off, I reached inside the plastic covering, and I touched his hand. He immediately latched onto my finger and started holding it. I was hooked from that point on. I started to talk to him and sing to him, and he knew that his daddy was there. He was so small. He was nineteen inches, long and he weighed six pounds and eleven ounces. I was in love again. I spent about an hour with Craig Junior. and then went back upstairs to check on Chrissy after she got some rest. When I got back up to the fifth floor, Chrissy was feeling a little bit better, and she was so anxious to meet and see Craig Junior. She hadn't seen him yet except when Dr. Foster stopped, and I took that picture. She was very emotional and nervous to say the least, but she was in so much pain. She had to wait until the following day to go down to visit him. She was about to see her first child. I helped her out of bed and into a wheelchair, and we headed for the elevator.

The closer we got to Craig Junior's room, the more nervous she got. I encouraged her and told her to be prepared for what he had on. I told her that everything was all right. We got even closer. I held her hand and she squeezed my hand tighter and tighter as we came to his door. When we got inside, we both just cried as we looked at him. His appearance to Chrissy was breathtaking, even with all of the tubes and wires, and I assured her that he was doing all right. She couldn't get over how incredibly perfect he looked to us. We were also very curious to see whether he was born with Down syndrome or not. We looked for those markers that they spoke to us about. The upward slanted almond shaped eyes, the crease on his hands, and the sandal foot. We physically examined him ourselves, and he had the almond shaped eyes, but so does my entire family. He didn't have the crease in his hands, but he did have the sandal foot.

The doctor told us that they were going to keep Craig Junior in the NICU for a few days with hopes that the hole in his heart closes on his own. To be honest with you, the only thing we were concerned about at this point was his heart. We could deal with everything else. We remembered what they told us about him possibly having to have open-heart surgery to repair the hole in his heart, so we were very concerned about that. Each day, Chrissy felt better from her cesarean section. We spent a ton of time on the NICU floor with Craig Junior, and we were pleased with his progress. He was eating pretty well, and we got a chance to feed him a number of times. It was a process, though, because he had all of the wires and tubes still connected to him. However, it was such a great feeling for both of us to hold him and feed him. He seemed so tiny to me.

I loved going from floor to floor to see him and Chrissy, but I felt at home when we all were in the same room together. I spent two nights in the hospital with them. I was exhausted, but I wasn't worried about me. I was only worried about my wife and newborn son. My older son, Dante', lived with us at the time, and he was at home with my mom. He couldn't wait to see his little brother. My mother brought him to see Craig Junior, and he was in awe of his little brother. My mom loved holding Craig Junior as well. She couldn't believe how precious he was. He had some other visitors as well that week. We made sure everyone that entered his room washed their hands prior to holding him.

On Monday, April 14, I met with the genetics doctor to confirm whether he was born with Down syndrome or not. There were two ways they could verify this for us. Either through a physical exam or through blood work. The doctor did a physical exam on Craig Junior, and based on what she saw, she diagnosed him with Down syndrome. We then left his room and went up to break the news to Chrissy. The amniocentesis prepared us for this very day. It gave us time to think about life raising a child with Down syndrome. We did a lot of research and knew what we were facing. When we got to the room, Chrissy was awake, and the doctor introduced herself and then told her about the physical exam. Chrissy's eyes welled up with tears as expected, but as I stated before, our main area of concern was his heart. Chrissy was discharged from the hospital a few days later, and it made things a bit more difficult for us since we had to leave Craig Junior in the NICU.

We went to see him every day, and we spent hours at the hospital then went home in the evening. Almost a week after Craig Junior was born, we got the phone call we had been waiting for. Dr. Foster called us one morning and told us that they ran some tests, and it has been determined that the hole in his heart has now closed. We were so excited! I felt a ton of pressure lifted off of me, so much pressure that I broke down and cried uncontrollably. They were tears of joy as I rejoiced my son and his journey. Chrissy and I held each other and cried together, assuring each other that things would be all right. We had a long road ahead of us, but we were determined to raise our son to have a great, quality life.

For the first year of his life, we were very busy. Craig Junior had many doctor appointments to go to. He had to see his pediatrician, he had follow-up visits with the cardiologist, and he had to see the geneticist, the neurologist, and the hematologist. We thought to ourselves, *Oh my goodness, will these appointments ever end?* Eventually, they all started to reduce due to the fact that Craig Junior started to beat all the odds. His appointments with his pediatrician were going well. He no longer had to see the hematologist. His follow-up with the cardiologist went very well and heart surgery was not needed. In October of 2014, Craig Junior was diagnosed with torticollis by his neurologist. Torticollis and plagiocephaly create upper body asymmetry that can prevent symmetrical neck extension and bilateral and rolling to the involved side.

This could, later on in life, affect Craig Junior's crawling, reaching, and sitting activities. The doctor also identified Craig Junior's abnormal head shape and face due to the torticollis and plagiocephaly. Based on this diagnosis, we had a small window of opportunity to be able to reshape his head and face with the use of a Cranio Remolding Orthosis. He now had to wear a plastic helmet twenty-three hours a day for the next six months. This process would reshape his head and remold him back to a more normal symmetry. This was a tougher point in our lives than it was for Craig Junior. He wore that helmet, and it didn't seem to bother him at all, but as parents, we know that society can be cruel. Whenever we went places, we would always get people staring at him or little kids speaking out loud talking about him. We built thick skin through this process, and we wanted to show our son that this may be what you will have to face in life, but you must keep moving.

Craig Junior was and still is very resilient and strong-minded. He was always such a nice little boy. He would waive and say "hi" to everyone he saw. He is such a kind kid. Finally, the day came where we could retire Craig Junior's helmet, and we were so thrilled with the results of his remolding. See, the torticollis began in the womb, the doctor stated. He favored a certain side in the womb and that is the side he was comfortable with when he was born. Since he favored a certain side, he would always lie that way when his skull was still developing, and he still had his soft spot, so we had to remold his head and face prior to his soft spot closing. It was all worth it.

Right after we were able to remove his helmet, we wanted to get involved with a local Down syndrome organization in the Tampa Bay area. We wanted to network with other parents that had a child just like ours. I Googled Down Syndrome Tampa, and the first organization that came up was F.R.I.E.N.D.S. The acronym stands for Families Raising, Inspiring, Educating, and Networking for Down Syndrome. I wanted to do a fundraiser at my job for this organization in October in honor of Down Syndrome Awareness Month. I called up the president of the organization and explained to her that I wanted to help and do a fundraiser for them. She was excited, but she told me she wasn't sure whether or not the organization was going to be open much longer. I told her, "Of course you'll be open, this is going to be great." Then I went on telling her all of the great things I had planned. Her attitude shifted to a positive outlook. We got off of the phone, and a day or two later, she called me back and asked me to meet her for lunch. I accepted. I also brought a copy of my autobiography called *Sharing Life, Sharing Moments*. I told her that I wrote a chapter in the book about Craig Junior called "Junior's Journey" that I thought she would find interesting.

While at lunch, she asked me to join the board of directors for the organization as the vice president. She asked me if I could put together our major fundraiser called the "Buddy Walk." I gladly accepted. I spoke with my wife, and we both were excited to be a part of this organization. We ended up having a great fundraiser at my job in October 2015. We invited people to bring their families— we had free giveaways, games for the kids, and free refreshments as we spread the word about Down syndrome during Down Syndrome Awareness Month. We ended up raising just under $1,300, and it was all donated to the F.R.I.E.N.D.S. organization. What a great feeling that was, and the president of F.R.I.E.N.D.S. West Florida (FDSWF) was thrilled, and she was reenergized now that I had joined as her vice president.

It is important to mention here that my main motivation and the reason why I had thrown myself into this organization was always my son, Craig Junior. He continued to improve and progress through his development. He went through times where his physical developmental delay was apparent. He had a tough time learning how to crawl and walk. They were both delayed for him, but through physical therapy, he accomplished both. He was so excited the first time he took a few steps. We got very emotional seeing his success. He didn't walk until he was about eighteen months old. He also has a verbal delay even though he has been in speech therapy since he was less than a year old. He is able to speak through sign language and verbally. He does get frustrated at times when he wants to express himself, but he can't speak the words to do so. He is a very bright kid, though. We speak to him in full sentences, and he can fully understand what you are saying. He will continue with speech therapy for as long as he needs to.

In 2016, I started to organize our first annual Buddy Walk. Our yearly operating cost to run our organization was about $4,000, and we had less than that in the bank at the time. However, the president of the organization asked me to organize this walk, and I thought we might as well do it in a big way. With any event that you are planning, one of the main things you need to consider is the venue. That was the big question—where will we hold the Buddy Walk at? The first place that came to mind was Raymond James Stadium where the Tampa Bay Buccaneers play.

I met with David Moss, who is the director of events for the Tampa Sports Authority, which owns the stadium and told him what our organization is about and what I was trying to plan for our walk. He gave me a tour of the stadium, and we worked out all of the particulars. In order to rent the stadium, the cost was actually more than what we had in our bank account. I had to now convince our president to trust the fact that we will raise the funds and more in order to put on a great event for our Down syndrome community. She was very nervous, but she let me proceed. I set a goal to raise $50,000 our first year, and after all of the teams and walkers and sponsors got on board, we ended up having about two thousand people attend the Buddy Walk, and we raised just under $40,000. It was incredible. I appeared on Tampa Bay's Morning Blend with Natalie Taylor (Allen), which is a local event news show on the ABC affiliate here in Tampa, and many people saw Craig Junior and I on the show. We had such a great turnout.

That set the stage for the second annual Buddy Walk in 2017. I was able to reserve Raymond James Stadium once again for the walk, and I continued to work with David Moss at the Tampa Sports Authority. This year, our goal was set at $75,000. I told the president that even if we fall a bit short of our goal, we will still finish raising more funds than we did last year. Everyone involved was super excited about preparing for the Buddy Walk this year. This is the one day that we all can get together and fight for the common cause during Down Syndrome Awareness Month. It's a great time and a wonderful event. In order to spread the word and get as much exposure as possible, I reached out to Natalie Taylor (Allen) once again from Tampa Bay's Morning Blend. I asked her if she could have us back on the show again to promote our second annual Buddy Walk and she welcomed us back with open arms. Our Son, Craig Junior, and I, appeared on the show, and it went very well. We got a ton of positive feedback and were able to get our event some publicity.

The co-host of the show that day was Roxanne Wilder, who is the radio host on Q105. During the break, I introduced myself and my family to Roxanne and asked her if it were possible for me to come on her show to promote the walk, and she said, "Absolutely." We exchanged information, and we set up the interview, and Roxanne was able to air the interview on four different radio stations for promotional purposes. I couldn't believe how blessed we were for both Roxanne Wilder and Natalie Taylor (Allen)to help us spread the word.

On August 11, 2017, I received an email from a new member that is a true example of why we wrote this book. The email was sent to the FDSWF inbox on our Facebook page, and it brought my wife and I to tears. This is what it says:

> A story I wanted to share about your appearance last year on the Tampa Morning Blend show promoting the Buddy Walk: I had my amniocentesis the day before that segment appeared on TV to confirm Sara's suspected Down syndrome diagnosis. After I watched that, with tears streaming down my face, I knew everything was going to be ok. Our family was 3 of the 2000+ people who walked into Raymond James stadium last year, and we are so excited to walk this year as a family of 4 now with Sara, our amazing miracle, who will be 9 months old at the time of the walk. This event truly makes a difference!

After I wiped my eyes several times and spoke with my wife at length, we spoke about this email, and this confirms why we were touched and inspired to write this book and share our stories. When we reach out to our Down syndrome community, and everyone listens, lives can be saved. This is why we do what we do. While our fight for our son, Craig Junior, is gratifying, we are even more empowered by our ability to serve other individuals who were born with Down syndrome.

At this point in his life, Craig Junior has beaten many odds that were stacked against him. He is a true warrior, and though still has a long road to go, he has come so far. On August 10, 2017, at three years old, Craig Junior started preschool for the first time. The experience on day one was one to never forget. Craig Junior was so excited to put on his uniform and go to school. Chrissy took things very hard. Being an educator, she knows the struggles he may have in school, and this was the first time that other adults were responsible for our son besides our mothers. What an emotional day. We got him dressed and took him to school. He sat outside right next to his teacher like a big boy. He looked like he belonged.

As they waited for the rest of his classmates, he sat there patiently and didn't cause any problems. At 7:45 a.m. it was time for the class to go back to the cafeteria for breakfast. Chrissy and I walked back with them. Craig Junior didn't want to walk back there at first, but the teacher's aide picked him up and carried him for about twenty feet. He then got down and walked with the rest of the class. I think separation anxiety started to kick in for not only Craig Junior, but also his mommy! We got into the cafeteria, and he got in line with the rest of the class to pick out what he wanted to eat. They came back to their tables, he sat down, and he started eating. He looked back at us, and he knew we were still there but gave me a look as if he was saying that it was okay for us to leave.

We took a few more pictures, and then I said to Chrissy, "Now is the perfect time to leave." We walked over to him and told him we were leaving, and I kissed him on his cheek. We closed the door behind us, and Chrissy took one last look inside the cafeteria at Junior and she started to weep. This was one of the toughest things she ever had to do. She cried so hard she almost started to hyperventilate. She started to collect herself as I continued to talk her through this situation, and she began to feel a bit better. He made it—three years old and in preschool, when we were told that he may *not* have a good quality of life. Our *hero* had beaten all the odds thus far and was here. We have never been so proud to be a part of the 10 percent of parents that made the *right decision*! We can't imagine not having Craig Junior with us. He touches everyone he comes in contact with.

His smile is infectious, and his personality is one of a kind. God doesn't make mistakes, and he sure didn't make one when he created our lovely son, Craig Junior.

After the FDSWF president disrespected me, I left the organization at the end of January 2018 and spoke with some other like-minded individuals about starting our own nonprofit Down syndrome organization. After a ton of planning and brainstorming, we formed Down Syndrome Association of Tampa Bay, 21 Strong. This organization involves some great folks with different backgrounds, and we all share the same passion of creating more awareness, education, and support for individuals Down syndrome. I was elected as executive director/president, and my wife, Christine, was voted in as the advocacy director. Lisa Mezzei was named our vice executive director, Robert Taylor brings his experience to the table as the director of events, and Kelly Taylor is our wonderful program coordinator. Tara Pitts was voted in as our secretary and Vanessa Hill is our co-secretary. Brittney Jones was named our transition advocate. Tanya Paisley joined us as our new treasurer, and we added Q102.5 The Bone's Drew Garabo as our new vice president and Rodney Fields and Verna Lewis to the board of directors.

Our organization hit Facebook in February 2018, and by April, we had over 3700 members all around the country. We strive to educate and advocate for individuals born with a little something extra with purpose, passion, and the utmost integrity. That is our mission statement and we hit the floor running.

Throughout the rest of this book, you will read stories from other families that are a part of the DSATB family. While most of our stories share a common thread, they are all unique. Please read all of our stories as we share our experiences with you in order for you to make the best decision for you and your family. Our experiences may be different than yours, but as you read our experiences, you can see how we all have had ups and downs, but in the end, the journey has been worth it.

God bless you, and may the heavens shine upon you!

The Mezzei Family

MY name is Lisa Mezzei, and I was thirty-five years old when Matthew was conceived. I was healthy, active, but still considered "advanced maternal age" by modern medical standards, having hit that magic number that sends OB/GYNs into a diagnostic testing frenzy. Agreeing to all noninvasive screenings, we found out that we were at a slightly elevated risk of our son having Trisomy 21 because his "long bones" were measuring a bit short on the ultrasound. Especially since we experienced a hard time conceiving our daughter, now nearly three years old and full of energy, and dealt with the loss of two babies via miscarriage (no chromosomal or other abnormalities found), we had no interest in putting this pregnancy at risk with amniocentesis or CVS sampling, both recommended to us by the perinatologist. Our faith was, and is, such that we would not have terminated regardless of any findings. We chose to live life, pray, and enjoy our daughter and this pregnancy.

Although there was no prenatal diagnosis, I "knew" right before he was born and was terrified. At thirty-six weeks pregnant, I woke up in the middle of the night with the knowledge our son had Down syndrome. Plodding to my comfy spot on the sofa, with my coziest blanket, I curled into a fetal position and wept. I stayed there for hours, until my husband, bleary-eyed and confused at finding me in such a state, found me when he woke to get ready for work. Through choked sobs and erratic breathing, I finally told him that what I believed to be true. Comforting me as best he could, thinking this was strictly a case of pre-natal anxiety, lack of sleep and hormones, he left for work. Arriving home ten hours later, he found me in much the same place, which was so far out of character that he wanted to call 911. Strictly out of pride and being unwilling to leave my house in a state of despair, I promised I was okay and went to bed for the night. Around thirty hours later, nearly a month before my due date, my water broke at 2:00 a.m. on a Sunday. After calling the OB's service, gathering a sleepy toddler and our fifty-five-pound rescue dog, we headed to my in-laws' house to drop them off and then made our way to the hospital.

Upon our arrival, I proceeded to inform every staff member from reception to the nursing staff, even the on-call OB, that our son had Down syndrome. Each one had the same reaction, followed by a flip through the file, which made no mention of what I was stating as fact, gave a confused look to my husband, who simply shrugged, and then patted my arm, and said, "Okay." To this day, I believe they all thought I was crazy. After just a couple of hours of active labor, our five-pound baby boy was born. Declaring him healthy, just little, we were assured he showed no signs of Trisomy 21. Once the staff cleared out, and it was just hubby, Matthew, and me, I told my husband they were wrong. Looking into my sweet boy's sleepy face, it was also then that I realized it didn't matter, and we were all going to be just fine. Me, with the crazy off-the-charts genius mother, who grew up thinking IQ was the most important measure of someone's worth. Me, the woman who hates attention, would now be getting attention for having a baby that was "different."

After a twenty-four-hour period, mourning the loss of my "normal" son, I put my analyst hat back on, my warrior mom hat on, and did my research. What to do, what to expect, how to give my child every advantage over the statistics? And guess what, somewhere among the negativity, I fell in love. Deeply! Madly! Forever in love with my son! And I realized he was the answer to my prayers, my dreams, and exactly the person I needed in my life. He is the only one that made me see, truly get, what is important. Despite my delusion to the contrary, striving for perfection gets you nowhere. And there is nothing perfect in this world but God. Aha! Guess who greets me with sincere love every time he sees me? Guess who is the first one to cheer his classmates when they succeed? Guess who is the only one to notice the cashier at Publix got a haircut? Guess who is the first to notice when someone needs a hug, or just a laugh? And guess who delivers it? So as technology advances and barely pregnant women are able to discover they may be carrying a baby with "genetic abnormalities," I worry other parents will never know this very special joy we feel every day.

If asked, would I say he is a challenge? Is it hard? I would say with every ounce in me *yes*! But so is raising his "gifted" sister to whom things come so easily. I could also say with all honesty that he is a joy, a blessing, and he makes everyone around him better people. How many people can we say that about? He has had the benefit of dedicated parents, a role model big sister, physical therapy, occupational therapy, speech therapy, teachers who believed in him, a stable home life, and very good health. He will be whatever, whomever he sets out to be, without limits. People want specifics, what to expect. I cannot tell you what your experience will end up being. Every child I have ever met is an individual. I can tell you that Matthew walked at eighteen months, was fully potty trained at three and a half years, read sight words at five years, and read chapter books (answered reading compression questions) at seven. He attended a VE (varying exceptionalities) preschool within an elementary school, general education for kindergarten, and first grade; and he has been homeschooled ever since. He thrived in every environment, made friends easily, and was happy.

We have tried some unproven (not enough funding for research) practices such as a neurodevelopmentalist, nutritional supplements, and QRI cold laser therapy that have been very beneficial; and some "proven" devices that were not helpful to him at all, such as orthotic foot/shoe inserts and hearing aids. My only recommendation is to find out as much as you can, ask other parents, try what you can afford, and just trust your instincts. We observe, pay attention, and make adjustments as one would with any child. Currently, he is an eleven-year old boy that loves cars, Nerf gun wars, Minecraft, playing jokes on his loved ones, reading, laughing, baseball, gymnastics, science experiments, family game nights, and ketchup.

He has proven the saying, "More alike, than different." Perhaps he has retained a childlike innocence a little longer than his peers, but I think that makes him fortunate. He forgives a bit easier and loves more unconditionally, both qualities we could all aspire to reach. As with every parent worth their salt, we research and question, stay consistent, make him accountable for his behavior, and cheer every victory—the big and the small. The journey is different than we may have set out on when we decided to become parents; it's better, we are better. Matthew makes us better. The emotional IQ he was born with is higher than the vast percentage of typical adults and more significant than any standardized test would judge him. He innately understands what many fail to see, what is important: kindness, courtesy, love, and fun.

The Quinn Family

My name is Jennifer Quinn, and I have a very unique story to share. In the fall of 2012, my husband and I were at a crossroads. We had two nearly grown children and had grown tired of our current routine. We prayed one evening for God to give us direction, purpose. That same evening, I contacted a woman on Craigslist about a water filter and arranged to meet her the following day. When I approached her door, I had no idea how that moment would change my life forever! She opened the door, and I was greeted immediately by a young boy with Down syndrome. He leapt into my arms and hugged me tightly. She apologized and moved to separate her son from my neck. I assured her he was just fine and that it was the best greeting I had ever received in anyone's home! She was followed by two more young boys with Down syndrome. We spoke for three hours that day, and she told me all about her journey to adopt all three boys from an institution in Ukraine. I was overjoyed and fascinated by these sweet, genuine, loving children, and knew that God had answered our prayer!

I shared her story and a webpage called *Reecesrainbow.org* with my husband as soon as I arrived home. Reece's Rainbow is an adoption site to help find children with Down syndrome and other special needs families. I didn't know how he would react and reminded myself to talk slowly and have patience for his feelings. The next day, I noticed my husband on his laptop and asked what he was doing. He said, "I am on Reece's Rainbow, I want to do *this*! I want to adopt a child with Down syndrome!" We immediately began research and decided to try for a biological child and adopt. We would raise them together.

Just ten months later, In August of 2013, our son, Gage, was born. He was a beautiful, healthy, typical baby boy! In October 2013, we began the process to adopt a baby boy with Down syndrome, Dunham. We traveled to Ukraine in the spring of 2014 and adopted not one, but two little boys with Down syndrome! Only five months after bringing home our two amazing boys, we felt the call to return to Ukraine and adopt a little girl with DS. We had seen so many children in need. We had the time, the ability, and the desire to help as many children as we could! In the winter of 2015, my husband traveled alone to Ukraine to adopt our beautiful daughter, Lettie Jean. Lettie had Down syndrome and a heart condition. She was strikingly beautiful with blonde hair and crystal blue eyes. We fell madly in love! We also adopted our son, Bogdan. He was four years old and had cerebral palsy, epilepsy, and hydrocephalus. Certain we were done adopting, we started a new business, built a new home, and settled in with our crew of five! Life was not without challenges, but not once did we regret our decision to share our lives with our adopted kiddos.

We tackled heart, brain, eye, and nerve surgeries together. We embarked into the world of therapy and specialists, and it was hard at times, but always rewarding and always worth it! In the summer of 2016, we decided once again to adopt, we wanted a sister for our only daughter, Lettie. In the winter of 2017, we brought home our second daughter, Annaleigh! She was eighteen months old with

Down syndrome and a heart repair. She fit right in, and she and Lettie are best friends! Our four boys keep us on our toes, and our two girls are always bringing sunshine. We share our lives, our biological son's childhood, our home, and our love, our everything with four incredible children with Down syndrome. It isn't always easy, but it is worth it! They make us smile and laugh, and their accomplishments give us joy and purpose.

I am in contact with our daughter, Annaleigh's, mother. We message back and forth on Facebook. She recently shared that she gave up her daughter because in her country, having a child with Down syndrome is shameful and not accepted. She told me and my husband that I had given her such peace and joy knowing their daughter was loved, accepted, and wanted. She was so grateful we continue to share our lives and her daughter's life openly with her. I am so grateful she is candid and honest and open to my questions. Life is full of hard things. I was an unwed teen when I gave birth to my oldest child. Each of life's teachable moments has many possible outcomes. I will never regret that I chose life for my child when I was a teen. I am so grateful that all of our adopted children had parents that chose life. I am grateful the Lord gave us wisdom and strength to step in and give the gift of a family to our adopted children. But their biological parents had already given them the greatest gift they would ever receive, *life*.

The Myers Family

Our journey from Tallia to Tia. It was around the time my husband and I were married for nearly a decade. We had each been working on our careers, trying to buy a house, and taking care of family. I had been working in special education and had finally finished school. My husband was working on his job for several years, and it was progressing well. We felt the time was right to have a baby.

After looking at others, we wondered how this process would be for ourselves. We were elated to learn that I was pregnant. We ended up at the doctor's office, where we find out, medically speaking, that I'd be considered an "older mother." As an older mother with my first pregnancy, the doctor recommended that we have prenatal genetic testing done. A few days later, we got the call and the results were in. We went back to the doctor's office where we heard words that would forever change our lives, "According to our genetic testing, your daughter has Down syndrome."

Everything else faded to the background, and the only thing I could think of was, "She's a girl…she's a girl! We will name her Tallia Ava!" I was thinking about the pink icing I would put inside my gender reveal cake for a future still-to-be-planned baby shower. I tried to focus in the doctor's office, realizing this was a pivotal moment, and I heard her wanting to confirm their initial diagnosis with an amniocentesis. She referred me to a specialist, and we were on our way, not realizing exactly how our lives would change.

Later, I was talking to my husband about his thought process in that room, and he also couldn't focus on anything in particular, but he remembers thinking, *Down syndrome, really?* He was trying figure out who was the Down syndrome carrier. Was it from his side of the family or mine? (Not that it mattered.) The truth is, we weren't sure, but we weren't the only ones. Even the doctors didn't know the fact that syndrome implies it comes from an unknown origin.

At the specialist's office, I was slightly overwhelmed with the amount of medical terminology and procedures that they wanted to do. I was asked about termination of the pregnancy, which, due to our background and beliefs, we had never remotely considered. We were still unaware of a lot of the challenges, but it was that day that the severe medical challenges my daughter would face really hit us. Up to this point, we had only been thinking of challenges to her education due to my background in the school system.

It was a long and emotional day, realizing that there is a serious medical component to having a child with Down syndrome. The words, "chances," "probability," and "likelihood," never had such a profound negative effect on us as they did that day. We informed the specialist that she was our first child, my mother's first grandchild, and only the second girl to be born on my husband's side of the family. We were extremely ecstatic and would be keeping our baby, but we still had some tough choices ahead.

I was about five months along, and we told the specialist that we did not want a procedure done just to confirm their diagnosis of Down syndrome, especially if it were to put the baby at risk. We decided to wait until she was born to meet our bundle of joy, and at that point, they could confirm their diagnosis. One evening, when I was further along, I was watching the news; workers who were supposed to be taking care of a special needs child were actually bullying and harassing him. Again, it was an emotional day, as I realized not everyone in the world was going to view my child as a blessing. I remembered my training in the educational system, and without saying too much, *I've seen some things.*

It was about the time where we really started thinking about what a day in the life of our daughter would be like. What challenges would she face? What kind of skills would she need? How could she get the most out of her life? Due to my background, I've always been a very large advocate of early childhood education. But I realized that her emotional well-being also needed to be cared for as well. She was going to have so many other challenges, and we needed to do everything in our power as her parents to minimize unnecessary challenges. *That's when we decided that we could not name her Tallia,* although it was a very important meaning for me it may have been too much for her. That's when we decided we would name her Tia because she was really a Tia.

With that mind-set, we had changed a lot of our original perceptions of what our first child was going to be and how she's going to live, to a more realistic, obtainable, manageable goals and hopes for her. But at the same time, we didn't just settle, we wanted the best for her. We're not sure how other people would handle the news, this is just our story. It's a complicated process and a very personal one.

Truth be told (we cheated a bit), I had both a traditional doctor and a Doula. Tia Josie arrived on her due date (to the day). She was born naturally. Kangaroo crawl. She was able to stay in our maternity room and didn't have to be admitted into the NICU. Things were going according to plan, but then the doctors, with somber faces, begun speaking. They told us, "She has Down syndrome." "We know." "And a hole in her heart." Our hearts felt that hole. Here we go, this is not a drill. It's time to hit the ground running.

That was two years ago. Today, Tia Josie spends her days waving "hello" to "her people," which includes her friends from her play-group. She has therapists and specialists. We have gone through hel-mets, braces, and walkers, but it has been worthwhile. She is our daughter, and we are "her people," or more emphatically, we are her parents.

So, bottom-line, if someone were to ask me, "Would you have a child who has Down syndrome?" my answer would be, "Yes." Or more precisely, the same as the first day the doctors first told me about Tia, *Oh, my God, she's a girl, I can't wait!*

The McGee Family

Our story about Sara. Many different traits can be found on a third twenty-first chromosome—Love, joy, strength, persistence, courage, and stubbornness are all present. One thing found on that third twenty-first chromosome that most people do not realize exists is *magic*. I know this to be true because Sara's story is nothing short of magical.

I was about fourteen weeks pregnant with our second child. Not many people knew that we were expecting yet, but the news was starting to spread at work. I had just gone into work at the hospital for a weekend of call, and one of the nurses on the floor approached me that morning during rounds to congratulate me on my pregnancy. She then proceeded to relay a story about her recently losing a pregnancy—turns out she had been expecting a little girl with Down syndrome, but it just wasn't meant to be.

At first, I was angry that she somehow felt compelled to share this information with me (myself being a pregnant woman who had just recently made it out of my first trimester and into the "safe" zone). My anger then turned into fear, and eventually to curiosity. I went home that evening, and the first thing I said to my husband was, "I think there might be something wrong with the baby." I then proceeded to repeat my nurse friend's story of losing her baby, emphasizing that the baby had Down syndrome, and also feeling as though we were somehow kindred spirits because we were the same age. He, of course, told me I needed to relax, and that I was completely overreacting. After all, I was only thirty-five, and we knew plenty of women older than us who had carried completely healthy babies.

No matter how hard I tried to forget this nurse's story, the thoughts that there might be something wrong with our baby continued to creep into my head every few days. I went to my sixteen-week OB appointment, determined to have some kind of genetic testing performed, but changed my mind at the last minute because I didn't want to deal with the hassle of obtaining insurance authorization for the testing, and also because I had convinced myself that these intrusive thoughts were, in fact, ridiculous.

The appointment that we had been waiting so long for arrived on August 31, 2016—our anatomy scan where we got the opportunity to "see" our baby and peek at his or her cute little features and take home our first official baby photos. We had decided we were not going to find out the sex since we hadn't with our first daughter either. I could tell that there was something wrong about halfway through the ultrasound when the technician appeared to be taking quite a few additional pictures of the baby's heart. I told myself that I was being paranoid, that she probably just couldn't successfully get all of the views she needed, but there was a definite shift in the mood in that dark room. We waited for what seemed like an eternity in the exam room in the doctor's office, waiting for her to go over the ultrasound with us. I again said to my husband, "I think there's something wrong with the baby. That ultrasound technician was taking way too many pictures of the baby's heart. Something isn't right." He put on a brave face and told me I was probably overreacting again, but I could see in his eyes that he was worried as well.

When my OB came into that exam room, she immediately cut to the chase and said, "The purpose of the anatomy scan at the half-way point of pregnancy is to view all of the major organ systems in the body to evaluate for any abnormalities. Unfortunately, we found an abnormality in your baby's heart. Your baby has a congenital heart defect called an atrioventricular septal defect. It is concerning because it is a defect that is commonly seen in babies with chromo-somal abnormalities such as Down syndrome." There it was. I tried not to look stunned. I tried not to cry, or hyperventilate, or panic. I tried so hard to process everything the doctor was telling us after that point, but I just couldn't focus on anything other than the words "Down syndrome."

My OB referred us to a Maternal Fetal Medicine physician for a more advanced ultrasound in addition to a fetal echocardio-gram. That appointment was scheduled for September 8, 2016. The night before my appointment, I was relaxing in bed and surfing the Internet. I opened up the Facebook application on my phone, and the first story that appeared in my newsfeed was a story that one of my friends had "liked" about an adult woman with Down syndrome who had made a significant impact in her community. It was at that moment that I knew with 100 percent certainty in my gut that our baby had Down syndrome.

The appointment the following day was relatively uneventful. The MFM doctor reviewed the level 2 ultrasound and fetal echo-cardiogram, confirmed the presence of the heart defect, and also informed us of a couple of other anatomical markers that were con-sistent with Down syndrome. He told us that based on the findings, he would give us a greater than 60 percent chance of the baby having Down syndrome. He also informed us that we were having a little girl. Even though I already knew deep down that she had Down syndrome, I still elected to proceed with an amniocentesis because I needed the information. Nothing would change our decision to con-tinue with the pregnancy, I just needed to know absolutely. Because of the amniocentesis, I took the following day off of work as instructed by the MFM doctor. That morning, I was relaxing watching television, and a segment came on Tampa Bay's "Morning Blend" show about the inaugural Buddy Walk being hosted by F.R.I.E.N.D.S. West Florida to raise awareness about Down syndrome. The segment featured Craig Woodard Sr., the vice president of F.R.I.E.N.D.S. at the time, and his then two-year old son, Craig Junior, who happens to have Down syndrome. I watched that segment with tears, streaming down my face, because I knew in that moment that everything was going to be all right. It might not be easy, but we weren't walking the path alone, and it appeared we were in very good company.

My doctor called me with the results of my amniocentesis three days later, confirming what we already knew. The events leading up to this moment are completely unexplainable by any rationality. I suppose you could call each of those instances complete coincidence, but I'm not sure that complete coincidences can occur that many times. I firmly believe it's the magic on that third twenty-first chromosome that spoke to me from the time I was fourteen weeks pregnant, preparing me to welcome my beautiful Sara with a little something extra. She chose me to be her mom, and though I don't always understand why, I know that I'm the most capable woman for the job, and that she's been preparing me all along.

I wish I could say that the road has been totally smooth sailing ever since, but that would be a total fabrication. As I mentioned previously, there are many traits found on that third twenty-first chromosome. The next trait that I had the opportunity to learn about is stubbornness. Sara spent much of the remainder of my pregnancy hanging out in a breech position, which resulted in me being scheduled for a C-section at thirty-nine weeks. I really didn't want to have a C-section, as I had had my first daughter vaginally, and recovered quite quickly from my delivery with her. As luck would have it, around thirty-six weeks, Sara flipped to head down, and my scheduled C-section was changed to a scheduled induction. I was ecstatic!

The morning of January 7, 2017, I began having early signs of labor, and by that night, we were headed to the hospital to meet our little girl. After we had gotten settled in, my cervix was checked, and the doctor ordered an ultrasound because she thought she felt feet. She was absolutely right. Sara had gone back to breech presentation, and we were headed to the OR at 3:15 a.m., much to my disappointment. I was learning very early on that I was just along for the ride—Sara was determined to enter the world her way. At 3:45 a.m. on January 8, 2017, Sara Darlene McGee entered the world via C-section, weighing six pounds thirteen ounces. She was born right at thirty-eight weeks, her way.

The next several months were probably the most difficult of my life, and it was during this period of time I learned about the strength and courage that are found on that third twenty-first chromosome. I know how significant they are because without those characteristics, Sara may not have survived. I've always been very hesitant to share our story out of concern that instead of providing new and expectant parents with hope and joy, it might evoke feelings of uncertainty and fear. The truth is, there can be many health issues that occur with Down syndrome, but then again, there can also be very few health concerns. Sara was born with an additional health condition that is seen in Down syndrome called Hirschsprung's disease, and she underwent a couple of surgeries shortly after birth to correct the problem. She, unfortunately, suffered several complications secondary to these surgeries, and it was these complications that resulted in her poor health early on, not Down syndrome. However, because she has Down syndrome, she was blessed with the fighting spirit needed to overcome all of her health hurdles early on. She underwent open-heart surgery on June 1, 2017, to correct her congenital heart defect, and she has been unstoppable ever since.

At one year into this journey, I have discovered the love, joy, persistence, bravery, and patience that are present on that third twenty-first chromosome. Sara brings the most amazing spirit and joy to our family, and she truly completes us and makes us better people. Despite all of her medical issues early on, she has been the most easygoing, content, and happy baby—far easier to parent than her neurotypical four-year-old sister. She has taken each and every challenge thrown at her in stride and carefully worked her way through it to reach the other side. In addition to completing our family, she has brought the most amazing support network of people into our lives to show us how wonderful loving someone with Down syndrome can be. We have a whole new extended family in our lives that we otherwise would have never known if it hadn't been for Sara. Do challenges still lie ahead? Absolutely. But those challenges would exist with raising any child, not just a child with Down syndrome.

I can't imagine my life without Sara in it, and I know without a shadow of a doubt that she is making the world a brighter place each day she is on this earth. The impacts that she makes are far-reaching. She has taught doctors that you can't judge a person by her diagnosis, and she has taught the family members in her life so many lessons already, including how important it is to slow down and take nothing for granted. I can't wait to see what the future has in store for her and our family. There are no limits to what she can contribute to this world.

Megan McGee resides in Plant City, Florida, with her husband, David, and daughters, Erin (four) and Sara (one).

The Bach Family

There is a theory that states that the earth and moon were once combined. Billions of years ago an asteroid or a meteor crashed into the planet. The impact, apart from causing a large chunk to break free, also generated enough energy to leave the two pieces molten enough to form back into spheres. As the Moon settled into its orbit around the Earth, it was responsible for two dramatic effects—the first being the well-known motion of the tides. The second was its effect on the shift along the axis as earth orbits the sun. Mars has no satellite to balance it, and its shift is 90 degrees. This would make weather patterns and climate very inhospitable to any life that might try to take shape. With the balance provided by the moon, the earth became friendlier to the potential for life and at some point, it happened.

This started me thinking about parents I saw at the store with their adult child with Down syndrome. I had always heard that Down syndrome kids were full of love and happiness and despite the challenges were a blessing to the parents. The child provides a balance to the parents in ways other kids cannot. I have no idea if it is correct or not, but it is an idea that passed through my head.

Now I find myself in the position being the parent of a little moon. I have no idea what lies ahead or what challenges we face. I will wait and see what his abilities are, what the differences and similarities to his older siblings are, what health issues he may have due to his condition, and how smart he will be. All the hopes and possibilities are going to be different for him than the other children.

And now I would like to tell you a little story about Alex.

Did you know that belly buttons can pop out? Because I sure didn't. But let me go back and set up the story that lead to this learning experience.

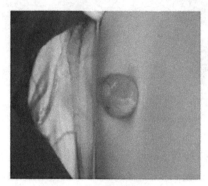

Alex's belly button.

It was a Friday evening after normal business hours, this kind of stuff always happens after hours. Anyway, I was home, watching Alex, while Mommy was out. It was bath night, so after dinner, it was time to get clean. Alex enjoys his bath. He can sit in his tub and play with the stream of water and try to grab the droplets. While he enjoys most of the time playing in the water, he doesn't like the water running down his face when his hair gets rinsed. After about fifteen minutes, I let the water drain and wrapped him in a towel to take him to the changing table. I dried him off and put a fresh diaper on him and noticed the inside of belly button looked a little red and maybe dirt was in there as well. I thought to myself, *That dirt is probably irritating his skin, I should clean it out a little better.*

Now Alex had always been an "outie" when it came to belly buttons, but I wasn't prepared for what was about to happen. I began the process of trying to dig into the small crevices while holding the belly button in place with my fingers. Thinking I had cleaned enough, I pulled my hands away, and his belly button looked a little different. Keep in mind this whole time Alex wasn't showing any signs of pain or the anything was amiss. But now his belly button was enlarged and redder than when I started cleaning.

Well, about this time, Mommy comes home. And as you can imagine, she was surprised by what she saw and expressed her "concern" with what had happened. I explained the best I could about what I had done. But the belly button remained red and swollen. So, it's off to the Internet to see what can cause this. I would like to take this opportunity to say the Internet can be a useful tool in finding out information, but it can also be scary—*very scary.*

Using "protruding belly button" as the search term, the result comes back "Umbilical Hernia." Did I mention Mommy was "concerned" earlier? Well, after reading that an umbilical hernia is the protrusion of the intestine through a small hole in the lining requiring surgery, and that I may have caused it, she was less than thrilled. And with the newfound Internet information a trip to the emergency room was required.

It was already late on a Friday, so I drove Alex to the hospital while Mommy stayed home with the kids. We checked in, and they asked some basic questions. Afterward, we took a seat and waited. A short time later, Alex was called in for the preliminary examination, and everything checked out normal, except the belly button. We were asked to wait again to be assigned a room. When it became available, we were escorted back to the room where I was finally able to put Alex to bed.

I phoned Mommy to update her, but there was really no new information yet. By this time, it was past midnight. Not being able sleep, I sat back in one of the chairs and watched Alex. The attending physician showed up to exam Alex. I explained what had happened as he inspected the belly button. He put his hand under his chin, and a perplexed look took over his face as he said, "I've never seen that before."

"So, it doesn't look like an umbilical hernia?" I asked.

He replied, "No, the hernia looks different. I'm not sure about this."

He ordered an x-ray to verify that it wasn't a hernia. But before the x-ray, the surgeon's assistant came to examine Alex. She looked him over as I explained the story once again and exclaimed, "I've never seen this before."

I said, "If I am bringing a new condition they can learn from, am I entitled to a discount?" Okay, maybe I didn't say it, but I was thinking it.

They took the x-rays, and the physician came back to show me the pictures. The intestinal wall was intact, and the intestines were where they should be. Yay for Alex, he was okay! Except his belly button was out. It was around 5:00 a.m., but they wanted to wait for the surgeon to see Alex before releasing him. His shift was scheduled to start in a couple of hours. I asked if I could take Alex home and come back since we live close to the hospital, but they wouldn't let me.

And then it was back to waiting. I let Mommy know it wasn't a hernia and that the surgeon would need to see him before Alex could be discharged. After a brief nap and some breakfast for me and Alex, the surgeon came in for his examination. He concluded that the belly button just became inverted and looked a little irritated. We discussed potential surgery to get it back to normal, and he said to schedule a follow up in month to determine the course of action. I thanked the surgeon, checked out, and took Alex home.

About a week later, Alex was rolling around on his stomach, and his belly button got pushed back into its normal position. Everything was back to normal. And that was Alex's story about an outie that became an even bigger outie. I told this story to a coworker, and they said, "I can pop my belly button out. Do you want to see?"

"No!"

The Miner Family

My name is Melissa. I was thirty-seven years old when I found out I was pregnant, again. My husband, Tim, and I already had four children. We had only ever planned on four children, so this was a surprise. My OB office, that had delivered my last two children, had moved out of the area and switched hospitals, so I had to find a new OB that was close to home and would deliver at the hospital close to me. At my first visit, when I was thirteen weeks along, the tech did a sonogram to take initial measurements to establish gestational age.

As she scanned my abdomen, she commented, "Wow, your uterus is very big for having four children." I wasn't sure how to react to that other than to say "Um, thanks?" Then as she scanned some more, she found another baby. I was having twins! Another surprise. The measurements seemed to take quite a bit longer than usual. Baby "A" wasn't in an ideal position, and the tech was having a hard time getting one particular measurement and spent twenty minutes trying to get it. After the scan, I met with the OB in his office. This was a first for me, as every other time I ever met with a doctor, it was in an exam room. He informed me that because of my age (over thirty-five) and because I was having twins, I was considered "high-risk." He also said that the measurement of baby "A's" neck was larger than normal, which was an indicator for Down syndrome. (I later learned this was called the posterior nuchal skin fold.) He literally threw his hands in the air and said, "I'm not going to touch you." He referred me to the only high-risk OB in my county, located at All Children's Hospital, which was an hour away from my home.

When I was home telling my husband everything that the doctor had said, I was more upset about his lack of bedside manner than the information he gave me. Additionally, since the tech had so much trouble getting the nuchal fold measurement, I wasn't confident that it was accurate. As a result, we didn't put much thought into the possibility of Down syndrome. As my pregnancy continued, the new high-risk OB office requested that I have an amniocentesis because of the abnormal measurement. I was told that the risk of miscarriage from an amnio is higher with twins, so I declined the test. They gave me another option, the Harmony test, which only required a blood draw from my arm and was of no risk to the babies. They explained that it would test my DNA as well as the DNA of each baby, combined.

The results came back saying that there was a 99 percent chance that one of the three of us had Down syndrome. However, the doctor said that because there were three sets of DNA, the test was not 100 percent accurate. I really didn't know for sure what to believe. I am very much a "we'll cross that bridge when we come to it" type of person, so after discussing the test results with Tim, we both decided that we wouldn't worry about it until the babies were born, and we could get an official diagnosis. I researched online how having a baby with Down syndrome could change the birth experience that I was expecting since I had already given birth four times before. I wanted to know if I should expect anything different. Would I have to have a C-section? Would the baby have to go to the NICU? Would the baby have to stay at the hospital longer? Would I have to go home without my baby?

The OB office monitored the twin's hearts very closely during the pregnancy. I had weekly sonograms and a more intensive sonogram just focused on the baby's hearts. Nothing was ever abnormal on the scans. There weren't any other markers of Down syndrome other than the original neck measurement. The doctors and I were confident that I was going to give birth to two very healthy little girls. When the day finally came for them to arrive, as I was in labor at the hospital, the thought came to me that it might be a good idea for me to save the babies cord blood.

I had never stored any of my other baby's cord blood before, but I had read that some children with Down syndrome have a higher risk of Leukemia. My thinking was that if one of the babies really did have Down syndrome, then maybe we could store the cord blood of the other baby just in case. I had never looked into cord blood storage beforehand, and apparently it's very expensive. The labor and delivery nurse told me that if we opened the blood storage collection kit that I would be charged for it. We decided not to open it until we were sure that one of the babies had Down syndrome. As baby "A," my daughter, Jessica, was born with the same OB nurse—that I had discussed cord blood with, and she was delivering her because they couldn't find the doctor in time. Immediately after birth, before baby "B" was even born, the delivery nurse turned to another nurse in the room and said, "Open the box." I was officially told that I had a child with Down syndrome by three little words—*open the box.*

Jessica, my daughter with Down syndrome, was born at thirty-seven weeks. She weighed seven pounds seven ounces, with her typical twin sister, Lillian, following four minutes later at seven pounds even. Thirty-seven weeks is considered full term for twins, and seven pounds each is considered very large for twin babies. Since all of my singleton babies were over nine pounds, I expected to have big babies. I've never had gestational diabetes, I just have big babies.

Having a baby with Down syndrome did not change my pregnancy much. I got to have weekly photo sessions of my babies in utero, and I had to drive to a doctor further away that I would have liked. But, all in all, I would say that was a pretty even trade. After the twins were born, they said there was no need for Jessica to go into the NICU, all her Apgar scores were perfect. They brought her into the nursery to run a few cardiac tests just to make sure everything was good with her heart. I didn't have to stay at the hospital any longer than usual, and I was able to bring both of my babies home with me when I left, no one had to stay behind.

I felt very blessed. I had these two brand-new beautiful baby girls to bring home to my other three daughters and son—one with Down syndrome and one without. Other than a few small markers, most people really couldn't tell the difference between the two—even my husband. Jessica has the almond shaped eyes that most people with Down syndrome have. Her ears are smaller and lower set, and one has a slight fold at the top. I call it her lucky ear (from Nemo). She has tiny white spots in the colored part of her eyes, which were much more noticeable when she was an infant than they are now.

I have to really look for them to see them now. She has a tiny little button nose. She has a larger space between her big toe and smaller toes on each foot. Her tongue stuck out of her mouth most of the time as a baby (tongue thrust). She does have excess skin at the back of her neck, which just so happens to be the softest spot of her entire body and my favorite place to kiss her. For me and Tim, the only difference between our twin girls is Lillian was born with hair, and Jessica was born without.

After we brought the girls home from the hospital, and they had their initial visit with our pediatrician, we were referred to several specialists. The first was the cardiologist (heart doctor). Jessica was born with a PDA (Patent Ductus Arteriosus) and ASD (Atrial Septal Defect). We only had to visit the cardiologist twice, an initial visit and then again at six months. Both issues had resolved themselves by the time she was six months old. She was released from Cardiology.

Next came the ophthalmologist (eye doctor). Jessica was born with cataracts in both eyes that needed to be surgically removed. So, she had two surgeries, one at one month old and one at two months old, to remove the cataracts. In order to remove the cataracts, the doctor had to remove the entire lens from the eye. Usually, in adults with cataracts, they immediately replace the lens with an artificial lens. The risk for glaucoma in infants is much higher, so they prefer to wait years before putting in an artificial lens. After the surgeries, Jessica essentially couldn't see because she had no lens in her eye to focus the light to the back of her eye. We are not born knowing how to see. Our brains have to learn how to see. So, it was very important that we help Jessica to see properly as quickly as possible, so her vision would develop normally. We tried glasses, but the prescription was so large, and the lenses were so thick that they touched her eyes. Not to mention, trying to keep glasses on a two-month-old was just not working. Every time she moved her head, they would fall out of position. So, we got her contacts. Yes, our two-month-old baby wore contact lenses, and she wore them for two years.

Once I got over my own heebie jeebies of putting contacts in her eyes and taking them out, it became just another part of our routine. They were not disposable contacts. She would wear them six days in and then one day out to give her eyes a chance to "breathe" and me a chance to clean the lenses. This worked great. We very rarely lost a lens, which was good because they were $150 each. At the age of two, she learned how to play peek-a-boo. As she would cover up her eyes with her hands, she would accidentally pop out her contacts. In one month, we had to buy three sets of contacts, so we went back to glasses. Unfortunately, we ran into the same issues that we had the first go around with glasses. The lenses were just too thick, and they were always touching her eyes or eyelashes, and she would not keep the glasses on. That's when we decided, along with the ophthalmologist, to go ahead and do the artificial lens implant surgeries. Each eye had to be done separately, and the surgeries were both successful. She now has glasses that we are trying to get her used to wearing, but the prescription is very small. They are bifocals and will be more important for her to wear when she starts learning to read and write in school. She will continue to be monitored by her ophthalmologist throughout her life.

Jessica took two hearing tests at the hospital when she was born. She passed in one ear and failed in the other. Then, the next day, she passed in the other ear and failed in the first one. They referred her to audiology. Children with Down syndrome tend to have very small ear canals, so trying to get an accurate result of the hearing tests was proving difficult. We did many hearing tests over her first year. The results were often inconclusive. Sometimes, it's hard to get the response you are looking for from a baby. They found that she had fluid behind her eardrums, so they referred her to an ENT (ear, nose, and throat) specialist. The ENT put tubes in her ears to drain the fluid. They ordered an ABR (Auditory Brain Response) hearing test, which she passed with flying colors! Jessica can hear just fine! She is still being monitored by the ENT, and her tubes have since fallen out.

When the twins were about six months old, we were at SeaWorld in the hot Florida heat in the middle of summer. I noticed that Jessica's chest was rising and falling more dramatically than usual with each breath. I wasn't sure if her breathing was labored, if it was just the heat, or if it was because she had a stuffy nose. That's one downside to having such a cute button nose—it gets stuffy easily. So, when we got home, I took her to the doctor who referred her to a pulmonologist (lung doctor). Jessica had developed a stridor—a high-pitched, whistling sound most often heard while taking in a breath. The pulmonologist did a bronchoscopy on Jessica to find out why. Jessica was then diagnosed with Laryngomalacia. Babies born with Down syndrome tend to have low tone or appear floppy. This just meant that her larynx was floppy as well. She outgrew the condition by the time she was one.

Jessica started with an Early Steps program from the time she was two months old. An Early Steps interventionist came to our home once a week to work with Jessica and I to help Jessica stay on track with her milestones. Babies with Down syndrome don't always follow typical timelines for milestones such a sitting up, crawling, and walking, so the added support is always helpful. Her ESI and I would come up with goals that we wanted to help Jessica work on and then she would show me things I could do with Jessica to help her work toward these goals. Sometimes, she would bring in a consult from speech, occupational therapy, or physical therapy depending on the goal(s) we were working on. Jessica began sitting up unassisted at twelve months, crawling before age two, and walking on her own a month after she turned three. Early Steps continued working with Jessica until her third birthday.

She then transferred into a blended three-year-old class (half of the students are typical, and the other half have IEP's) where she receives additional services in speech, occupational therapy, and physical therapy. She has only been at school for two months now but is doing so well. She is picking up new things daily and is learning so much. She uses a reverse posture walker at school to help her walk from the classroom to the cafeteria or PE. Even though she is walking independently now, she is much faster with the walker and can keep up with her class much better.

Jessica and her twin have been watching sign language videos from the time they were big enough to sit in high chairs. Jessica, for the most part, is nonverbal still but uses signs and word approximations to communicate. These last six months she's really grown in her speech therapy class at All Children's Hospital and is trying to repeat and sign more and more words. It's amazing to see how fast she is picking things up. She loves books and loves to be read to. She loves songs that include hand signals like "Itsy Bitsy Spider" and "Twinkle, Twinkle Little Star." She will ask repeatedly to read a book or sing a song. She memorizes both fairly quickly and will read and sing them with you.

We didn't plan to have six children, and we certainly didn't plan to have a child with Down syndrome, but I wouldn't have it any other way. I'm so thankful that God gave Jessica to us. She has taught us so much as a family in her short three years. She is teaching my older children about kindness, compassion, and acceptance. I love that my children want to be active in the Down syndrome community because of Jessica. She has taught us as parents not to be afraid of the unknown. She has brought so much joy into our house. She is such a sweet little girl. I'm looking forward to all the wonderful things she will accomplish in her life, and I am blessed that I get to share this journey with her.

The Decision

We hope that after reading the many different stories shared by all of these wonderful families, that we have touched you in a positive way. We *all* were in your shoes and, most importantly, we understand how you are feeling. We all had different journeys, different paths, and unique adventures. We shared our life experiences with you so that you could make *the decision* to create great experiences of your own. We have found that our children are gifts from up above. They are truly remarkable, and they enlighten our lives each and every day.

You will go through some tough times, different ranges of emotions, but just know that when the dust settles, the sun is shining on the other side. The Down Syndrome Association of Tampa Bay is not only here for the Down syndrome community in the Tampa Bay area, we are here for the *entire* Down syndrome community and hope that through our stories, you have found strength, comfort, and love. For more information or if you'd just like more support, please reach out to us by visiting our website at www.dsatb.org, email us at craig.woodard@dsatb.org, follow us on Facebook at 21StrongForever, on Twitter at DSATB.21Strong, or you can call us at (814) 882-9191.

Many Thanks

There are many people that I'd like to thank for helping make this book reality. The idea of writing this book as a group came to me in the summer of 2017. I presented the idea of board members sharing their stories, writing a chapter, and letting the world into their lives with the hopes of reducing the termination rate post genetic testing. A 90 percent termination rate is extremely high, and there is a strong possibility that some of those terminated births were children who were not going to be born with Down syndrome. The board members liked the proposal, and they have all come together with me to send a strong unified message to all readers. We wanted to educate, uplift, and let you all know that it will be all right. So, I'd like to begin thanking all of the coauthors of this book starting with Lisa Mezzei.

I would like to thank D.S.A.T.B. vice executive director and treasurer, Lisa Mezzei, for sharing your truly amazing story about Matthew. You and your family have played a huge role in the success of our organization, and your story will touch the lives of many. Thank you for always being there. I appreciate your talent, experience, and kind heart more than you know.

Thank you D.S.A.T.B. member, Jennifer Quinn, and her wonderful family. Your story about adopting four children born with Down syndrome is truly amazing. It gives a different perspective to parents and lets people know that there are great families out there that can provide a wonderful home for children. Thank you for being a part of this project.

Special thanks going out to D.S.A.T.B. members, Melissa and Tim Miner. Your story about the twins is magnificent. Jessica and Lillian are wonderful little youngsters, along with the rest of your beautiful family. Thank you both for being involved in our organization and sharing your life with all readers.

Thank you D.S.A.T.B. members, Megan and David McGee, I thank you all for telling us how seeing that there is support out there made your experience hopeful. Megan, I can remember the first time I read your e-mail about you watching Craig Junior and I on Tampa Bay's Morning Blend. When I read it, I broke down in tears. It touched my heart, and I was blessed for the fact that we reached you. Little Sara is an angel as well as Erin, and I thank you for sharing Sara's story with the world.

Thank you D.S.A.T.B. member, Lawrence Bach, for letting us into you and your family's world. Alex is a great young man and will do big things in his life. He is so blessed to have you and his mother as advocates, mentors, and parents.

D.S.A.T.B. members, Tahira and Travis Myers, I would like to thank you both for allowing us all to experience what you lived for a short period of time. Tia is a beautiful little angel, and I am so glad that you reached out to me and that you all are a part of this wonderful project.

I would like to thank many people who have helped D.S.A.T.B. become the great organization that we have become today. I can't forget thanking D.S.A.T.B. director of events and program coordinator, Robert and Kelly Taylor, respectfully and their wonderful kids, Caleb and Ansley Taylor. Beautiful family. Thank you all so much for everything you do to help keep this organization going. You both are full of ideas, and I appreciate working with you side by side.

Thank you, Tara Pitts, Vanessa Hill, Brittney Jones, Rodney Fields, Drew Garabo, Russell Lewis, Sr., Verna Lewis, Tamara Churchill and Alexis LaCrue, for joining the board. We truly appreciate your service.

Special thanks to Ashley Phelps for editing this book. You helped me edit my first book and were there for me once again. Thank you so much!

I would like to thank all our sponsors who help this organization financially. Special thanks to John Sullivan, Bryant Martinez, and the Winthrop Town Center for all you have done for us and continue to do. Also, I would like to thank Terry Johnson and the Winthrop Charter School for supporting us over the last few years. They have created awareness within their education community for Down syndrome, and I can't thank you all enough.

I would like to thank Nicole Bennett, Jeffrey Cooley, and Kaleena McQueen-Jones, and all from Ippolito Elementary for your support for Craig Junior and recognizing Down Syndrome Awareness.

Special thanks to Hillsborough County Superintendent, Jeff Eakins; Assistant Superintendent, Tracye Brown; ESE General Director, Kimberly Workman; and Pre-K Exceptional Education Supervisor, Joanne Manwaring.

Also, special thanks goes to Pinellas County Superintendent, Dr. Michael Greco and ESE Executive Director, Lynne Mowatt, and her team. The support in the education field is much appreciated.

I would like to thank my entire team at OneMain Financial all the way up to the head of the company. These are truly amazing people who support this cause and we are grateful.

I want to thank my mom, Sylvia "Be'" Woodard, and my father, Dr. Charles "Chick" Woodard, for all of your support, your help, and your upbringing. Your strength and love has allowed me to be the best father that I can be. I want to thank my two older boys, Dante' and Jordan Woodard. Boys, I am honored to be your dad, and I thank you both for being such good big brothers to Craig Junior.

I can't forget thanking my mother and father-in-law, Karen and Robert Erdley. Your support has been a blessing to us, and I appreciate all that you do.

Thank you to all the hospitals and doctors that pass out our organization information and refer patients to us as we extend our services to the community.

I would like to thank Tampa Bay's Morning Blend host Natalie Taylor (Allen) for all you have done over the years for us. Your generosity is appreciated. Thanks goes out to Q105 The Current's Roxanne Wilder. Your friendship and support is truly appreciated. I would also like to thank Fox 13's Walter Allen for supporting our cause as well.

Last, but not least, none of this would be possible without the love, support, and the great ideas from my wife, Christine Woodard. Chrissy, you give me strength when I am weak, and you have my back when I feel alone. Thank you for putting up with me and being there for me when I need you. Our story about Craig Junior was written from my perspective, and I know you saw some things a bit differently. I want you to know that I see a fantastic mother. I had no doubt you would be the best mom ever when Craig Junior was born. You are truly thoughtful and hardworking, and you are the glue that holds our family together. I love you and thank you for all you do.

If I missed anyone in my acknowledgments, please charge it to my head and not to my heart. I want to thank each and every single D.S.A.T.B. member out there. You all make us want to work hard for you and your children. Please spread the word and be proud of your kids. Stepping up and speaking about how our experiences were may just help someone else make it through their journey. As I stated before, about 90 percent of parents terminate after getting a diagnosis of Down syndrome from genetic testing. I hope this story helps you understand what you may be in store for and also lets you know that there are families out there who would love to adopt that special angel. Give your child a chance, the journey may be rough, but they will one day stand before you and say, *"I have "ThisAbility", not a disability."*

Special Thoughts

To all the little babies out there who never had the opportunity to prove to the world that they would someday be something special. We dedicate this book to those parents out there that may have been misinformed, scared, or uncertain of how things would turn out for their child. To those that felt they were doing the right thing by terminating the pregnancy after receiving a positive Down syndrome diagnosis. That is a tough situation to be in.

To the many parents that will be put in this same position in the future. We pray that this book reaches you in time so that you can see that you will be giving birth to an angel. To all those children that lost their lives after birth due to complications dealing with the pregnancy, we love you and know that you are our *guardian angels above!*

CRAIG WOODARD SR.

About the Author

Craig Woodard Sr. is a father, a loving husband, and the executive director and president of the Down Syndrome Association of Tampa Bay. He has written and published an autobiography called *Sharing Life, Sharing Moments*. He is a former TV sports anchor and former pro football player for the Erie Invaders. He has three boys and his youngest son, Craig Woodard Jr., was blessed with Down syndrome. Craig and his wife, Christine, are huge advocates for Craig Junior. This is his life, and he has set out to change the world one conversation at a time.

CPSIA information can be obtained
at www.ICGtesting.com
Printed in the USA
BVHW070956030220
571272BV00005B/591

9 781645 598329